THE HOUNDS OF NO

BY LARA GLENUM

Action Books
Tuscaloosa, Alabama
2005

Action Books
Joyelle McSweeney and Johannes Göransson, Editors
Jesper Göransson, Art Director
Kristina Sigler, Assistant Editor

Action Books gratefully acknowledges the support of the Office of the
Provost, College of Arts and Sciences, and Department of English at
the University of Alabama.

Action Books
University of Alabama, Dept of English
103 Morgan Hall, Box 870244
Tuscaloosa, AL 35487-0244

Learn more about us at www.actionbooks.org.

Library of Congress Control Number: 2005928196
First Edition

Cover Art by Lisa Hargon-Smith

for Jožka

CONTENTS

PRAYER IN THE TIME OF TERROR

O Lamb of God
O Ringleted Lamb,
　　　　skiddle-dee-deeing down the road! O bright-fleeced!
　　　　O Lamb
with your face so entirely
blown away

O Headless Lamb
with your three charcoal legs

O Bodiless Lamb
Lamb of Vapors
　　　　cooked and steaming on a silver platter
　　　　　　　　(This is my body, illuminated
　　　　　　　　by a sniper's nest —
　　　　　　　　This is
　　　　　　　　my skin, a pretty lace
　　　　　　　　　　　　of holes, stretched out in a doorway
　　　　　　　　　　　　to dry)

O Lord
We, the least ones,
saddled with flesh
　　　　jeweled with the shining shrapnel
　　　　of your face
We pray to you

O Little Lamb
Why can't we be like you
Headless
Eating clouds

EXCRESCENCE

outgrowth esp as result of disease or abnormality

O his creamy jets

    of   dime-store hypnosis

                    are

                  luscious and spoiling

        with a sweet poison that I slather on my

              neural interstices

              while

he drags his pink tongue over my   salt-caked spine. And O!

                    his sparkling

            cotillion of zeniths &

            fake rabbit skins! O his wicked

                 isotopes!

O his product-line of meaty heaving in snowpiles!

Meanwhile, his ribs burst open

     to reveal

     a golden button/icicle   which I

              press/eat until my pleasure-domes

                  cave in.

                  (And I,

            in a crystalline fervor, silver strings of saliva

            trailing

from my lips, kneel down while a diamond axe tumbles out of

the heavens

        to chop off

my head.)

And electronic birds

sing

all grizzly and parsimonious and the tight buds explode like ammunition

          in the creamy air.

     And then…. And then!

St. Liberata and the Alien Hordes

I was crucified   as an alien host!

    Still hanging on the cross   they peeled the seedy, white pods
    out of   my large muscle groups

    & scraped the sleeper colony out of my left lung

In Nicomedia, I'd been seen leading a winged devil by a chain
followed by a UFO

The hermaphroditic cults of Cyprus
said I was pursued   by aliens disguised as plague pigs
                  with tiny bells around their necks

    They carved
    strings of pods   like firecrackers   out of my spinal column

& The whole time
the executioners heard chattering noises   The hard shapes of antennae
could be seen   wriggling against the walls of grey amniotic sacs

In jail, I'd grown a beard   & wore shoes of solid gold:
      The Bride of Heaven!

Lumpy & swollen with a thousand pods   I began to split at the seams

             It was sheer ecstasy   until the high court
                        convened
Until the craven Emperor with his long, curling fingernails
      mandated that
        I be crucified
        before I erupted & gave birth   out of every
                      major organ

      out of every oil-gland
         & mucoid duct

WUNDERKAMMER

I was a meat-based creature I was chunky with carbon
I grew spleens, nails, fat-lobes, etc.

It all ended

I ascended into Heaven The angels sounded like high-
pitched techno wails Their spooky faces were all identical

One angel came forward & sank his fist into my stomach
as though it were a ball of wax He pulled out a dried-out
milk gland It looked like a tiny tumbleweed He then pulled
out: Two wigs A city A goat skeleton He mounted all these
on a styrofoam plaque He said, *Good job, buster*

He sent me back to earth

I sprouted eleven ovaries & nine penises I dangled edible
babies from greasy crimson stalks I wanted nothing more
than to be eaten alive & shat out Just like in the last life

I was later rewarded first prize at the angelic banquet for my
silvery leaves & cuckoo colonies

This time I'd been an exceptional plant

How to Discard the Life You've Now Ruined

Sneak into the "shame hole"
Remove the squirming pink sack from the gray pelt &
put a second body inside
Or hang the body from a telegraph wire that transmits instructions

To those who've drowned in an automatic wind
While choking on state-licensed vision cloths

Hang the loose skin in a weeping museum

Use the smallest bones as buttons
Sew the buttons onto your face & pose in several helmets

Or collect the larger bones & make a stylish 4' x 6' cage
Plant the nerve-cords in window-boxes
Let them trail down like vines outside your new home

In the evenings
Use the spine as a flute to play
the soft nationalistic marches of the "bodies without organs" collective

Carve tiny beasts out of the teeth & wrap them in strands of black hair
Sew the animals into your stomach
Advertise your crimes as "the failings of a zoo"

Tack the two legs onto your own hips &
gallop through zones of agony
Now you're a four-legged animal downed in the onslaught

You're a weeping brute clogging the light-hole
in the eye of the sun

Marlene Dietrich's Letter
to an Unidentified Admirer

:: [In a pixellated hearse: [the shrunken people who are [kept on strings : look out [onto
the [ignited air
of Berlin ::
[Around & around they drive : [trying to greet passersby [through
mouthfuls [of blood ::
[They shriek [at the serial flashes [of the paparazzi ::

:: [Their several strings
are tied [to a stake [driven through the center of [my chest ::   ::   ::

                                        ::

*[: In order to avoid them, I join a circus made of meat – The tent is sewn
out of the skins of the circus pigs – In my ring, I perch on a sofa made of
pork fat wearing a baroque wig & waving a cleaver – I try to coax the
winsome animals out of the chandeliers by coyly lifting my hoop skirts to
reveal the charcoal stubs of my legs :]*
                                 ::
::
In this [occult sadness
I hold a séance: for [the cameras :   : [whose lenses [melt all over my neo-
Egyptian gaze ::

                ::

*[: I am helping the handsome Nazi commandant to take the peninsula – In
a gold lamé headdress, I recline on a bed of stuffed asps while he toys with
my rodent-shaped mastectomy scars – In the final shot, I ascend a glass
ramp into the mouth of a statue of jackal-headed Anubis, pursued by the
Nazi commandant, whom I've placed in an occult trance ::]*
      ::   ::   ::

: [& Still there is :

::   :: [no report [of Victory   ::   ::
[Not even from the [Minister of Propaganda's flaming offices ::
     ::

:: [In the [end :
[There is only : [your idiotic head rolled to a stop [at my feet like a useless
     [ball of wire ::

                     ::   ::

:: OUT OF THE COFFIN I LEAP ::

Thousand-eyed, I spin : My skin dripping ::
Off me like pearlescent wax : In my cell ::

I slit the throats of the Choirboys of Anguish ::
I set the Flocks of Emergency free ::

Out of the coffin I leap : My skin like ::
A sheet of holes : The light pouring through ::
The holes like tar : Let the pearls of insurrection

Roll across the dead eye of God : I carve ::
The bleeding swan out of the ranks ::

Of my own electric flesh : Out of my own ::
Ivory breastbone : I am the relic of the new ::

Ivory megaphone : I sky the reliquary, too ::
Of my own trick-flesh : Clouds of my moan ::

The bleedings want out of the bank ::
Enroll in the dead-eyed School of Dog : I, larvated ::

Three voles in tar : Let the pearls of an erect sun ::
A bleat of gaols : The kites snoring through ::
Out of the cough, in I creep : My grin a pike ::

I clot, a box of emergent seas on my knee ::
I omit the bloats of the cowboys of English ::

Scarf me like pear-luscious wax : In my knell ::
Thou-and-I, I spin : My seashell crippling ::

16

Message to the Department of the Interior

I have decided to grow a second body This may be of some
concern to you

I fear my second body will have a forking spine & a rubber
leg & refuse to wear anything but a bloody deer costume

I fear my two bodies will have unseemly public duels

The second body will, in all likelihood, publish obscene
treatises on "the hairy halo" & radicalize the cottage industry
in deer pornography

It will most certainly attempt to cut off the face of the first
body & wear it as a mask whenever it enters "the reality
testing booth"

It will drool "red language" into a steel cup affixed to its chin
The "red language" will be collected & be inserted into the
tongue-holes of its enemies to induce morbid hallucinations

I know you said I should try to relax & ignore the residue the
bombs left in my torso

by eliminating all my bodies & proto-bodies, but who can
relax in our republic now that it's laid its terrible eggs on our
tongues

Snow-White in Versace

The glass coffin, it was clogged with hair. My meaty kept on growing.
The prince yanked me. My fingernails became a six-foot nest of

curl-i-ques. I was eight. I lived with seven men. Time had not been
butchered out successfully by the queen. The queen sighed,

embroidering on the tool of the king. Doodle-doo. The king gave queenie
a looking glass. To corset her milky eye into a fit. To absent her

from court life. *Here*, he cooed. The chunk of apple dislodged from her
shrieking crotch. The mirror, at least, had pity on the pearl-inlaid handle.

Of her sobbing knife. I did not. I offed her, the pleather-clad vixen.
With my crystalline nerve-coat. A jerking foxtrot. Diamond-tipped shoes.

A Diorama of My Pucelage

In the forest of ovaries, crimson trees snap beneath the weight of their egg sacs. With a large, pearl-covered button, I fasten the thick flaps of skin over the holes in my abdomen. There are hairy rivers I will not cross. Dolls climb backwards out of my mouth.

On skin-covered trees, colonies of embryos hang like crystal pendants. The Mother-body slides among them, a predatory spider, dropping mannequin legs out of her shiny thorax like silent bombs. I prop the mannequin legs against tree trunks, frilly socks slouching at their ankles.

The Mother-body lives in a black velveteen parlor littered with anesthesia canisters. As she works, glass figurines crowd around her macular hole. Raptor fetuses shriek toward her through the tired skies.

constant mentions of hairy?

The Mother-body sails the hairy rivers, scavenging. She will remove my poison sacs. She will remove the deposits of nougatine cream in my shriveled forelegs. I will wear her glass coffin like a wedding dress.

The Adela P. Kerduckian School for Well-Bred Young Ladies

We stood in line for weeks, just to master a single task. A centaur taught courses in gothic fetish at the bottom of the reflecting pool. A drill sergeant barked out orders: *Always leave a calling card when attending an afternoon massacre. White kid gloves should be worn at a funeral and should only be taken off to toy with the corpse. A jewel-encrusted abortion kit is always a fashionable gift for a female relative.* We watched the televised revolution in doily knitting. We learned how to decorate pig corpses with oily copper lipstick for the holiday feast.

All the while, we dreamt of the hyena-judges, of the nubile boys at the State Flesh Exhibition. Of eating case after case of meat popsicles and winning shiny trophies. The crystalline swamps of cock. The lines, though, they rarely moved. We stood stock-still for weeks.

In the control tower, the Mother-body eyed us on a monitor screen. Her three left breasts dripping milk into the stratosphere through a set of plastic tubes. As we failed task after task, her hands turned into piles of white feathers. And dispatched their miniature armies of infanticide.

A Treatise on the Affective Origins of Female Hysteria & Schizophrenia (ca. 1880)

Women, who have frail "Happy Way Bus Routes," who are easily carried away by the Quilligan Quail, by the lively movements of their own Key-Slapping Slippards, are more often attacked by nervous diseases[1] than Genghis Khan Schmitz, Horace P. Sweet or Butch Myers, who are all more "marshmallow-stuffed, full of shrieks, gone to pot." But this excess of irritation/vivacity[2] has a *peashooter*: that in the very midst of Pomplemoose Pass[3], it attenuates and frequently ends in Vent #5 (extinguishing the senses). The nervous system has such a bad case of the gleeks that it is then incapable of transmitting the soul to[4] the Boola Boo Ball; all its figures are disordered; it can no longer interpret its own tin-plated pants.

---

1. Notably, "Mice-in-the-Beak," "Glittering-Towers-in-the-Air," etc.
2. See Kohlfritz's piteous remarks on the three days he spent in "that bird-filled-up place."
3. Famed for its sparkling glass road, which leads directly from the genitals to the cranium.
4. *of transmitting the soul to*: A much-debated phrase. Some have translated it as "of stuffing the cock into," while other insist on "of candying the semiotics for."

In the Gynecological Museum

How I wish the lacy valentine had not been flocked out in
mongoose pelt! I'd never have come. I rode in on the horse named

Exhibit A. The doctor inoculated me against pink-eyed rabbits.
A key turned in my petticoats. "Your hair wants cutting," he said,

settling me into the stirrups. My legs withered as he settled me into
the fur-trimmed corset. Into eyelets & bone-rings. The good doctor

kept his hands in an ivory box. In the shop window of my
abdomen. Mannequins began cutting up the leaflets on hygiene &

loped off to the orphanage, brandishing axes. My tongue turned
into a hardened black stamen. When he told me that the golden

scapula was made from the führer's metal buttons, I ate my
Victorian bed hangings & overturned the chess board.

Off to teatime, I muttered, spitting out history like a terrible pill.

SLAINGUAGE

Who reeked of sutures & klepto-schooling?
Who pitched me headlong off the carousel
at the Happy Asp Petting Zoo?
                    *

                    *

                    *

                    * Eat my glissando,
            detective, & corroborate:
                    *

                *Who kept
dog-drooling at the beastly mezmerata
                        while
                I bleated, defective?
                Who shot

            the Saint w/the morphos
                in a bell jar
                    [*]
while he
kept screamily & forcing his way into
        the glass ark
            lined w/my vermilion, eel-slippery
                            skin?

The Manifestation of Male Hysteria

Mother wanted to stop and save her "jewel-case." But Father said, "I refuse to let myself and my children be burnt alive for the sake of your *jewel-case*."

This was surely just the situation to call up a distinct feeling of sexual excitement in a boy of fourteen who had never been approached.

The anorexic boy is a hyperbolic version of the slim, strong, active, accomplished young man our society admires.

The same boy – and now we see him through a soft-focus lens – frequently bursts into tears, lying in a flag-draped coffin, missing half his face.

To everyone in the parlor's surprise, the boy recounted numerous accounts of being seduced by "The General," who had presumably been impotent for decades.

The emergence of these disassociated visual memories produced a striking "ego-alien visual hallucination": oil wells sprouting out of the hysterical boy's own comely ass.

Male hysteria, with its "unique expressiveness" and "ability to symbolize distress in an alternate language," possesses the potential to slaughter tens of thousands in a matter of seconds.

Throughout the "cure," the boy was prone to spells of shallow volatile emotion, overdramatic behavior, susceptibility to suggestion, hysterical blindness, right-sided paralysis, and amnesia.

In sniper fire,
he was seemingly unresponsive to external stimuli and, in many cases, seemed to be living out a "vivid, hallucinated drama."

Especially characteristic of such episodes are the "glove and stocking" distribution of motor disturbances in the limbs and a refusal to do housework.

The hysterical fit, however, has been out of fashion for many years.

The Tale of the Wicked Lotuses

The Lotuses :
are vicious : Like pale bees in the veinlight ::
    They arrive in town
    discreetly :
toting their bag of needles : & check in at
          The Leaky Sun ::

They have their reasons : They have
their purposes :
(Don't ask unless you want to wear 1,000 needles
                    in each eye : & spend your life kneeling
                  on glass
        in a cloud-colored room :
    like some light-corroded Madonna) ::

The Lotuses
they see you : They coo like mangy doves ::
    They invite you into the Dark Shrine :
              & tempt you with Maiming :
      & a nice plate
      of milk ::

In private
they king you : They gobble you : They drain you ::
    At first
    it nearly tickles : like a candle in your daintiest pleasure :
            or a fragile cloud-song :
     & then the razor ::
     (& then you're missing your legs) ::

(I once ate
the Lotuses :: I ate them & ate them : until something Keen & Bright
        climbed out of the Lake of Static :
        to pick my bones clean) ::

In the Garden of Nails :
there are strange, milky flowers :
        All of them
        streaming : into the Sun :: When the Lotuses come at last
                        for you :
                You'll come out white, too ::

CZARINA OF THE SUPER-SACCHARINE

The bullet-shaped cloud fell into the shining lake's face.
I voted to detonate. I voted to Empire.

Vanilla, Vanilla!
the Ibis-headed men chimed, *You are our cathexis, our panoptikon.*
Entering you, there's no place
from which we are not seen. Eye of God & etc. They placed a zirconia
tiara on my head.

Excuse me, I said, *but in flaming mausoleums,*
my bones float in bowls of sulfuric acid, a sacrificial rite. The female body is a thousand-year-old
freak show of
dried-out mermaids. Excuse me, I said,
but my face is melting off
onto the stove eye.

O! Excuse us, Vanilla!
they demurred, bobbing their Ibis heads in unison, *May your baton lessons*
at last free a slave!
Excuse us, they chimed again, cocking
their pistols, *but may we*
at least touch the golden pin in your hip? Tin stars dropped into my lap & a jar
of clear jelly
was set out. I served them a round of
bullets, only it was too late.

Christ! The wise, old
(vivisected) rabbit muttered
on seeing my skeleton: *She is a palace of desiccated fetuses.*
[Weeping, they placed a call into Headquarters:
Vanilla, Vanilla, we have killed her! Our Lady of Silent Hemorrhages,
Our Atomic Empress,
her colonies have fallen! She is dead!]

CRUSHIFIX

We need some beef-relief. I think we'll drink
His cream. I think we'll starve & roseate
A morphic resonance the size (I think)
Of die. Swans can cream, too, inebriate

Of why. Do only we disjoin our lungs?
Will the howls overreach me before we
Can take off our skin & let it be hung
On a mannequin, spritely fitted? "I

Traffic no cadavers," said the owl
& ate my demi-monde. ("Why go trilling
Into? & spuriously creaming!?") Our skull-bowl
Is a fountain of electrodes, killing

Nothing, nothing. If he is swan & roseate,
We ovulate skeletons & language cremate.

STRANDED IN AN INDUSTRIAL WINTER, THE BODHISATTVA QUAN-YIN BEGINS TO SOLILOQUIZE

The porcelain clouds
hiss and drag.
    When I left, O Faceless,
it was the year of the Rat:
        crossing chemical-pink skies, crossing the cliffs
        of the thousand chrome buddhas, crossing
    aeons, I came here,
to where iron ore wails,
to where steel bridges twist like rogue spines
        over riverbeds.

The snow leopards
followed me here. Outside the uranium mines,
    the radishfields leak
    across the bleached leaves of the sun. There, the leopards feed.
Every day they grow leaner. Every noon
the snow
descends in flakes like human skin.

At the needle exchange clinic, the others say
you've failed to exist, but
    the mouths in my arm say, No —

        (At what distance, O Faceless, under what black jade heaven
        do you lie, sperm ticking
        like an atomic clock, while I continue seeking
            through these 10,000
        kingdoms of disease?)

When I ride again in the snake-carriage
  above the lands where the earth discards its pale horns,
                                        I will find you —
                                  Seeking

[The Manuscript of the Nine Corrosions, *as it is called, breaks off
here. However, a later version adds: 'Seeking, seeking, seeking!'
replied Faceless, 'There is nothing to be found.'*]

KRIEMHILDE & SOCK-MONKEY'S BUSY DAY

Dear Scientists –

My name is Kriemhilde. I am an inmate at the Admiral J. Sock-Monkey Correctional Facility.

In the courtyard, I whip the clouds until they scream birds. The clouds have leathery black tongues that loll down and drag across the earth, destroying Sock-Monkey's many homes and palaces.

Sock-Monkey is a piece of shit floating in the cosmic cream. He smoothes me out with a crowbar. He pleads, 'Kriemhilde, my child, relieve me. Suck the sputum out of my threadbare crotch.'

I pull off his little button-eyes and sew them onto the asshole of a pig.

Sock-Monkey wears the dried-out skins of his enemies as an apron whenever he bakes his famous pink cupcakes.

I *am* very interested in your experiments. I do own a baton. When do you visit?

Oedipus Sock-Monkey

I have a lavaliere of ghouls percolating in each of my pig-engines. I think
they belong to you. I think the recent convergence of museums and

execution chambers is the main reason that I continue to mistake you for a
bloody exhibit on totemic animal corpses instead of thinking of you as my

father. Your underwear is atrocious. The stains look like an intricate map of
an archipelago where the dead are trying to shove their faces up out of the

loamy ground. One of the faces is clearly mother's. Someday the lozenges of
crystal that you eternally weep will detonate at your feet, and then I will

finally inherit your kingdom, which I will promptly rename the Flea Palace.
Thank you for the bouquet of fists.

Oedipus Sock-Monkey II

Thank you for the drill set. I tried drilling extra orifices in my princess meat. In my abdomen, I found stalactites of dried-up semen & a dead pig lying beneath them. With tweezers, I tried to remove the shiny pearl from the dead pig's eye.

On detonation, red sugar spilled out of the corner of my mouth.

At the memorial service, I saw you wearing a tiara, lying in a body bag. The embryos inside you rode around on conveyor belts, shrieking with glee.

The man had nine penises. I failed to have enough openings. In the afterlife, how I hope that you will pass me by, at last mistaking me for a scorched, discarded femur.

Sock-Monkey's Treatise on the New Typography

O Meat Light
O Vulture Light   O Daughter
Detonated, I bleed sublexical characters & pink cartoon rabbits

In the new typography,
the sky will appear onstage in full war regalia
The horizon will be a thick caramel smear with bombs bubbling out

In the new typography,
severed limbs will be pasted onto the landscape
& letters will be planted like land mines in each of the Valentine substrates
O Parasite

The brain is a white alligator-skin suitcase full of grenades & ivory horns
I take the steel pin out of my neck
My lungs are an air-raid siren

Off falls my plastic head

In the new typography, the mutated deer will escape your mouth
& the embryos lodged in its antlers
will fire on me with machine guns

I will at last appear in the sun
The skin of vowels hanging off me in long strips

This is as it should be in the new typography
O Daughter

All my meat will be revealed
& All massacred Heaven shall see it together

KRIEMHILDE'S ARIA

I wrote an aria for you. Each note is inscribed on a sugar cube lodged in the hoof of a rabid pig. You may only sing it on days when you eat pornographic balloons and contract elephantitis and begin to repent. Repent!

Mother may be dead, but she is still watching you through her cloud-periscope. She sees the tapeworm between your legs drooling glue with grief whenever the herds of mastodon pass.

Hermaphrodite Sock-Monkey

I wore my crystalline nerve-coat
for the first
five days And a pig-skin candelabra
        for the rest
            The stuffed owls on the mantel exploded
I posed for the family portraitist
in my mask of plastic tubes

I need a plastic bag in which to hide the animal
        I need a wedding cake to sink my duplicate bodies
I need a pig skeleton
to hide my dainty oracle

(In that performance   I wore a kabuki mask
I spoke through the horror megaphone
        I blew powdered milk
into the black craters
where the language-babies keep breeding

I fed them cuckoo shit
And popped their shiny heads)

I cry I wake I cry I wake
I sockeye
I neoteny like larva   with precocious vulva &
        outrageous marble erections
Sphinx-like I suckle bombshells
at the gender-rendering farm but

Which performance am I   ballet or salvos

37

The Kriemhilde Chromosome Is Mutating

The term Sock-Monkey has been applied to certain morbid states of the nervous system.

And Jesus said: Things seen in a Kriemhilde are more certain than those we behold in dreams!

Shrill Kriemhildes of joy declare: Sock-Monkey! May your button-eyes multiply like flies all over your head! May the veil of red rubber tubes in your chest part to reveal the head of the slaughtered lamb!

Sock-Monkey said: I cut deep into her face so as to freely expose her. A quantity of clear water escaped, and with it, two or three small daughter cysts.

And Jesus admonished Sock-Monkey: You gave me no kiss, but from the time Kriemhilde came in, she has not stopped eyeing my cock.

The crouching Kriemhildes cling to the earth in a pallid ecstasy. Beams shoot from out the fairness of their slit. Sock-Monkey invents a cruel rack in the Tower of London to torture and force confession.

And Jesus said: The Kriemhildes are not sleeping but dead.

The Love-tale infected them.
Their buds penetrated the cyst wall and began to develop externally.

They danced on the shore, the Kriemhildes of the land.
The Kriemhildes and their hundred earls.

The Coveted Remains of St. Kriemhilde

A pair of dried-out ovaries dipped in gold

A necklace of teeth

The Vision Cloth [through which the oracular cream first spurted out of her
most holy seizure]

A pelvic bone [ground into a fine cosmetic powder, in 14 stoppered vials]

A platinum wig

A shattered cranial plate

A peg-leg [preserved in a tall glass case and decorated with golden figurines
of wily centaurs, drill bits, mannequin legs]

The skeleton of her pet goat

The Scientists' Instructions to Sock-Monkey

The nature of the experiment is such that you will grow a second head. The nature of the experiment is such that we will sew a glittering ball gown out of your intestinal membranes to outfit your young daughter. The nature of the experiment is such that you will finally be cradled in the decaying jaw of the Redeemer. The nature of the experiment is such that your wife will become a new form of artillery. You will say, 'Thank you.' You will be polite. The nature of the experiment is such that you will be shown pictures of your adolescent daughter lying naked & face-down on a flaming lawn, impaled on her own baton. You will be polite. You will not ask after her walrus. You will be polite. The nature of the experiment is such that you will be shown into Victorian elf factories and be forced to manufacture miniature crystal ornaments in the shape of ovaries. The nature of the experiment is such that you will no longer be a stupid doll.

A Diagram of Kriemhilde's Dollhouse

The Salon

The Mother-body chewing on
pig skeletons
under the gold divan

The Smoking Room

The heads of slaughtered lambs
fastened to metal plates

A nerve lantern

Lactating spider-girls

The Kitchen

Sock-Monkey in his apron
made from the skins of his
enemies
baking pink cupcakes

The Olive Bedroom

A cormorant
A calcified voice

The Puce Bedroom

Kriemhilde in a platinum wig
rolling around the room
inside a bloody amniotic sac
like a strangled kitten

A pair of shattered pig
stockings

The Attic

The Mother-body's spare plastic
parts

Sock-Monkey's recipe books &
pamphlets on typography

Kriemhilde's lovely (forsaken)
head

MEDIEVAL: :BESTIARY

O rocks, says the she-goat
to the cock,
I'd rather be skinned alive and nailed
to the barn door than
endure this spike of ache
in my gonads ::

    & Redbud to redbud shrieks
that the naked filaments of sap
      are licking out
        her insides: *I beg you*
Pick up a dried-out rat bone
Scrape me out ::

& Even the sky's pearl-throttled
engines
are choked with a demon seed — ::

    O yes O yes O—
    At Easter,
even Christ's alembic
is sucked clean ::
      & The self-flagellant
copulates with a white-hot iron
crying, *I alone*
am God's meat & The Noon-Witch flickers
    across the mallow-fields ::
    & The darkling sheep
      kneel down
at the baroque altar of their genitalia ::
    & In a tent
made out of Christ's flayed & tattooed skin
you & I
shriek out like
    semen-sluiced lilacs, erupting ::

THE HAIRIEST ROOM OF ALL

& There I was creaming fountains in the hairiest room of all
splayed onto the fingers of the Messiah positively dripping
onto his ivory wrist

My tattooed face was crushed like a lily against the hairiest of
walls & a mynah bird was recounting how the Messiah was
such an excellent taxidermist which I hardly believed

until the Messiah sliced me open & tossed my organs in a
glass beaker & crammed my torso with gobs of cotton &
dragged me out of the hairiest room of all

He stuck me in an overstuffed landscape with poorly
upholstered clouds (I could see the white seams showing on
all the trees)

& I said *Is this it*

& He positioned me among the sprightly forest creatures
my front hooves off the ground leaping back as though I
were in pain

but I wasn't I could feel nothing

CARVE A NICHE IN YOUR FLESH
& STORE YOUR SECRET PURCHASES INSIDE IT

A dangerous toy. Not for use by ballerinas shot in the face.
Clean clogged orifices with chainsaw/feather dipped in lye.

Plastic limbs are useful for catching birdshot. Do not act wicked
or do. Insert vermilion or spermatic fluid into slots J & I.

The razor-like part which maims is contained obsequiously
in jelly-like skin (with or without periscopic crotch-eye).

Tube of blue icing is for skying prettily at abominations. Keep
legs open. Do not eat head. Apply tape to mouth. Or mummify.

(Exiled fetus: $3.49 for 4 singles, $8.99 for triplet-twin mix.)
(Siamese twin version available at select boutiques in NY.)

Throne of iron nails, no. Telepathic pet rabbit, yes. Included.
Please recycle any laser-like interstices of sinusoidal joy.

ABORTED

On the horizon,
the albino sun drags the scratched-out land through
     the far gate
     of pearl.
        You say,
This life is stillborn, toting out a pair of dried-out ovaries
and a crucifix of spit. My days
        snap in two
               like fingerbones. In the ice-litter, the cherry trees
    shriek out, their anemic blossoms
       scalding the eye.

    In the valleys,
the clouds lie
like cracked porcelain dolls, bleeding into
     the radishfield refuse. Semen stains the mountaintops. You say,
             A single screw of flesh
             binds me
         to this life and to the pale fire
               beyond the veil.

In their jars,
the embryos float, each in its corona of nails,
    a bleak eye
        turned toward Heaven.

Sewage rings the sun,
and in it,
the embalmed angels circle like a haze of flies. The moths fly off
      to lay their eggs
    in a field of static. The ragged Fetuses of Light lean down
               from their coffins of lead
      in the clouds, hissing:
    Beware, beware.

Pornography

I flip the channel.
Pink O-ring. Pink baton.
The medical landscapes straggle through me,
        toting their abstractions.
White jets. Jellies and occlusions.
(In the far corner of the screen, on a wall crucifix, Jesus suffers
            the ecstasy of plastic.) Then — static, static.

> In the cracked shell of a TV
> lies a pile
> of dusty limbs
> and a single lotus.
> The lotus says: *No exit.*

No exit from these hieroglyphs
on the pavement of non-meaning.
No exit from a life circumscribed
by flame.

(I say: Like Hell.
I place white-out here, over the meaty celluloid that it may congest with sick stars.

I scratch out these skewed limbs
hanging on the tree of sight.

        I cut out chrome skies, pink anemones, chalk cliffs
and glue them onto the patient screen.

We are not bodies, we are nimbuses of static
seeking our starry capes of flesh.

And I, without you,
a moth
pinned alive.)

MARXISM WILL GIVE HEALTH TO THE SICK

I use my veins for leashes. At the end of each vein floats a snail, a pelvic bone, a car engine, an orchid. My pets hover above me like dangerous balloons. A crystal lozenge escapes the macular hole in my degenerating eye. We are walking. We are walking. Toward my hospital bed.

~

Look at these lifeless bones! These sugar-coated sacs of nerve. I did not wish to marry a pile of meat.

~

Drain a cornucopia of pig fat into my throat. I'll never get better. I lie under the planetary blanket. The skull medallion emerges on my forehead. Let the heads of my ancestors arrive on silver platters to bless me. Drill seven holes in this seashell. And drain the agonies out.

~

I said: I am several diseases singing in polyphony. I said: I am being slobbered on by the Hounds of No.

~

The sun vomits blood onto the Aztec pyramids. My veins twine in and out of the lace holes in my rococo wedding dress. The thickest lie in meaty coils about my throat and fork out. Into the coppery sky. Look: two aviators have gotten caught in the heretic branches. And the gibbous moon.

How to Obtain the Girl-Scout Badge for Succeeding in the Afterlife

:: I will travel the meat-paved road that leads to crystalline Heaven ::

:: When I arrive :   the Virgin of the Twenty Agonies
     will take out
my three souls :
She'll tie one on a string & give it to a cloud-demon for a pet :
Launder one and stamp it for reissue :
     The third
     she'll slice into tiny pieces & sew it deep :
into the loamy earth and   watch the screams come
         sprouting out of it   ::
         ::

:: The sky will roll itself up
like a scroll &
     a squadron of seraphim with blue reptilian tongues
in towering baroque wigs :   will dislodge my organs :
& place them in concrete urns
     inside a white dwarf to dry ::
     ::

:: & I'll wrap the blue cellophane sky   around my shoulders :
& I'll recline
     for an aeon   on the celestial expanse of pink shag carpet
     like Zsa Zsa Gabor on amphetamines :
& watch
the saints deepen behind the machines   ::   ::
       ::

     :: & No one will ever guess
that I died   the same as I lived   ::
with a sharp   ::
     string of tears hanging out of   one eye :
         hysterical and
        useless

The Name of the Ghoul

As the signified marched down to the harbor to embark, the
streets through which it passed were lined with corpse-like
effigies and exploding coffins, and the air was rent with the
noise of the machines wailing for their dead language.

The child first entered the Symbolic register upon learning
the name of the Ghoul.

Christ signifies "the void in all things." The floating signifier,
by whatever name it was known, was often represented, year
by year, by human victims slain on the harvest field.

The men slew the god of language, grinding his bones in a
mill, while the women wept crocodile tears.

Then the dead were believed to rise form their graves and go
about the streets, vainly endeavoring to enter temples and
dwellings, which were barred against these disturbed spirits
with ropes, buckthorn, pitch and siren-like sequences of non-
meaning.

When the Emperor Julian made his first entry into Antioch,
he found that even the gay, luxurious capital of the East was
plunged in mimic grief for the death of the signifier.

It is conjectured that the cross to which Christ was crucified
was actually language god's enormous wooden tongue.

MEDEA AND THE SNOW-ANGELS

The Golden Fleece! The Golden Fleece!
     he shrieked.

Get over it.
Get some sheep, I told him,
dismantling my tongue
     and laying the pieces out on the Aegean marble table. Already,
we had wasted
ten years. Already, thousands had died
at my hands.

Daily, Dread & Co.
kept moving all our candy-cane-striped furniture
off the ship.
Dead squirrels kept calling out to me from beneath the frozen tundra, advertising
     fake diamond jewelry.

That he had a silver-plated fork for
a tongue
was our gravest misfortune. I wrote to Stalin *Over the dead sea, the winter sky*
     is shredded into holes
I kept falling through.

In Mongolia, snow-blind, I became lost
in a maze of white.
(The walls of the maze were chock-full of miraculous creatures.
     Naked, male. Miraculous.)
In Sparta, I ate a piece of black licorice
and it turned into a larva. At an oracle in Ethiopia, a golden mask
     of the sun
told me to take up knitting.

I killed our children.
It kindled his desire.

I said, *Back, hornet! I am off*
with the scantily clad snow-angels!

Starting to cry, I said,
One by one,
they will lick each of
my blinding transgressions clean.

In the Tents of the Wicked

When he got down,
Barabas made a beautiful injun sit on his leg. *I put rouge on her boobs,*
he wrote in his diary, taping
      one of her canine teeth
to the page. To celebrate, he ate red velvet cake
and took in
a porno flick.

[*I fucked the mountain*, Barabas wrote. That the rock is a "she" is obvious. That he
didn't really fuck her, thank goodness, is the problem with sexualizing nature.
Or elves. Or anything that limps your way.]

On the Mount of Olives, Barabas
tied antlers
to the girl's head. He made her eat glass
        and mate with a man costumed as Quetzel-Quetal,
    the fierce Jaguar-Serpent god,
while lying on
a nest of scorpions. *A real Zapotec!* he cried
into the loudspeaker. He sold elk-skin moccasins by the thousands. In this way,
he lured people
    from all across the Valley of Jericho
      to his sideshow.

Soon after, the girl's eyes
turned into golden balls. Barabas started dreaming
    that he was lying on a pile of candy-canes, being eaten
by a white hyena
with genitals of ice. *You are doomed,*
      said the elders. *This is the curse of Quetzel-Quetal.*

[*Maybe it's not necessary*
to fuck
every knothole in the forest, Barabas wrote. The dead animals
                    by the side of the road
                    rejoiced, *Hooray!*]

After several seasons,
profits waned. Soon after, Barabas
was found
quite dead, strung up in a spiny acacia tree. In the Tattooed Lady's tent,
        the girl found
the skin of God
hidden away in a velvet box. Early mornings, she'd put it on
                        and run shrieking
                    through the dried-out riverbeds.

Funereal Landscape in Minerals

In this necropolis,
I am Queen.
        On the long, black-and-white tiled piazza, the shrieking statues
        tick out
the dull centuries. (In this kingdom of
                mineral half-breeds —
        the zinc seahorses, the pig-iron clouds — all nod to me.) Each noon,
                            the quartzite surf
                            thuds into
           the blind cove. For leagues around me, nothing else
        moves. Only the blindfolded castrato,
my sole
companion, sings to me
in shrill mimicry
        of the wind. On the horizon, the real wind
                halts, afraid.

On a craggy cliff face,
I sleep standing
in my robe of glass. Starless nights, I dream I am fleeing,
        stepping out
                onto the museum of the sea, among the obsidian dolphins,
                            frozen mid-leap,
                  the anemones littering
                the mica-encrusted shallows.
For a thousand years, I have woken to the sound of phantom ships
breaking up
against the reefs below, the cries of
        the ghostly crews.

Today, even
the mother-of-pearl sun
has rolled
        out of the sky, and, for the first time in eternity, it is
        snowing. By nightfall,
my antique
collection of statues and funereal sea-junk, the calcium cliffs —
           all will be deleted in a static of white.

I, Medusa,
am being buried alive in the mausoleum
              of my own gaze.

The Regime of Bliss

I am trying to lasso the diamond-inlaid missiles straight out of the sky
                                                                and

          to detonate all cakes
          iced with
          petrol/lemongrass frosting and kick the Troops of Death
                                                      in the leg
                              as they parade past in their candy-cane-striped pants
                                      en route to the film set/oasis
                                      and

                        to blithely
              shoot down the Hounds of No
                              with
                      a peashooter (as they arrive over the bleeding metropolis
                                      in bomber jets, gunning
                                      their dandelion engines)
                                      and

          to fling
          a Molotov cocktail
                  on behalf of all the secretly oppressed neural exchanges
                                              and
                                      the language exiles

                        It is all so sloppy!
              And I intend to be neat
              (or at least
              precise)
                      as I loudly play the leg-bone trumpet out over the fertile swamps
                                      of our collective misery

as I slough the dead cells
off
a sparkling set of aesthetics

and promote
outright
the Regime of Bliss.

APPENDIX

MANIFESTO OF THE ANTI-REAL

1. Art is neither a form of consolation nor a butler to hegemonies. Even in its most discreet moments, art explodes.

2. The Anti-Real does not deny the Real.[1] The Anti-Real knows that everything is in annihilation in the Sublime. The Anti-Real is that which seeks to manifest itself through the secret side-door to the Sublime rather than through the mock world of realism.

3. Realism is the bordello of those who would have their perceptions affirmed rather than dilated. When the door of fascism is opened, Realism will be seen lounging like a whore in its inner sanctum.

4. The Apocalypse is a way of thinking. Only the Apocalyptic clock announces from atop the grotesque pile of refuse, 'The Kingdom of Heaven is now.'

5. Irony is not a device. It is a state of being.

6. To be Anti-Real is not to be Surreal. The achievement of Surrealism lies in displacing correspondences, in the poem not arriving. In the Anti-Real, all assumptions are disabled, too, with one difference: the Anti-Real displaces causal logic with a totalizing logic of violence.

7. 'Defile! Defile!' shriek the Obliterati as they vandalize the museum of silence. Secretly, they, too, are wet-nurses to sentimentality.

8. Sentimentality is a form of exploitation, a connivance with official lies. Hang sentimentality on the gallows of Emergency.

---

1. Even though the Real does not exist.

ACKNOWLEDGEMENTS

I would like to thank the editors of the following journals in which a number of these poems initially appeared: *American Letters & Commentary, Black Warrior Review, The Canary, Conjunctions, Denver Quarterly, Diagram, Dragonfire, Fence, Hotel Amerika, La Petite Zine, LIT, New American Writing, Pleiades, Pom², Soft Targets* and *3rd Bed.*

I would also like to express my gratitude to all my teachers and peers in Chicago, Charlottesville, Prague, and Athens for their invaluable criticism and advice. Thanks in particular to Claudia Rankine for her exacting eye and to Jed Rasula for his tireless enthusiasm and generosity. I am especially indebted to Joyelle McSweeney and Johannes Göransson for their support and faith.

Thanks to my family, in all its constellations.

About the Author:

Lara Glenum was raised in the gothic South. She studied for her M.A. in English at the University of Chicago and received her M.F.A. in Creative Writing from The University of Virginia. In 2000, she received a Fulbright to Prague to translate 20th C. Czech poetry. At present, she teaches among the kudzu vines at The University of Georgia, where she is a Ph.D. candidate specializing in Modernism and the Historical Avant-Garde, post-modern aesthetics, and theories of the sublime and the grotesque. She lives in Athens, GA.

ACTION BOOKS TITLES 2005

Remainland: Selected Poems of Aase Berg
Scandinavian Series #1
Johannes Göransson, Translator
ISBN 0-9765692-0-5

The Hounds of No by Lara Glenum
ISBN 0-97656592-1-3

My Kafka Century by Arielle Greenberg
ISBN 0-9765692-2-1

www.actionbooks.org